15 SMART Board

Lessons for Tackling Tough-to-Teach

Grammar Skills

Jessica Ewert • Amy Lena • Susan Van Zile

New York • Toronto • London • Auckland • Sydney
New Delhi • Mexico City • Hong Kong • Buenos Aires

Teaching *Resources*

Acknowledgements

To my unforgettable students, who inspire, support, and teach me every single day. Their loving spirits continue to ignite my creativity and passion for life inside and outside of the classroom. To my husband Cody, for his masterful words of wisdom coupled with his natural sense of leadership and guidance. His endless love strengthens all of my endeavors. To my parents, Donna and Chuck, for teaching me to reach high and rise above all challenges. Their unconditional love and support continue to help me grow and achieve. To my dear friend, colleague, and mentor Susan Van Zile, who offers a remarkable perspective on life with advice and encouragement that are unmatched. Thanks for cheering me on!

—Jessica Ewert

To my husband Matt and two daughters, Maddison and Rylie, for their unconditional love and support in all that I do. To my parents, who have supported and encouraged me throughout all of my endeavors and have helped me achieve my dreams. To my sister, who is always there for me and inspires me to become a better person. To my dedicated colleague, Susan Van Zile, whose passion for teaching is inspiring to all those around her.

—Amy Lena

This book is dedicated to the Great Creator, who provides us with all that we have and all that we are. To those who teach and inspire children and to our beloved students, whose imaginations, enthusiasm, creativity, and vision solidify our common belief that in their hands our world will become a better place. To my beloved husband, children, and parents for their abiding love, support, encouragement, and understanding. To my passionate, dedicated colleague Jessica Ewert, whose creativity and enthusiasm for her students, life, and learning are unsurpassed. To Amy Lena, whose technological prowess and innovative design motivate and engage students. To Scholastic, for inspiring and nurturing children.

—Susan Van Zile

Editor: Maria L. Chang
Designer: Grafica Inc.
Illustrator: Mike Moran

Photo credits (for SMART files on CD): 4 Action Verbs: race cars © Doug James/Shutterstock; soccer player, skateboarder © iStockphoto; reading girl © Monkey Business Images/Shutterstock; 8 Confusing Verb Pairs: girl lying down © wavebreakmedia/ Shutterstock; students raising hands © Morgan Lane Photography/Shutterstock; setting table, brick layer, sunrise © iStockphoto; sitting girl © Big Stock Photo; 9 Common and Proper Nouns: Michael Phelps © Marka/SuperStock; New York skyline, angry adult © Big Stock Photo; book photographed by Lindsey Dekker; 13 Prepositional Phrases: laptop computer, pool © Big Stock Photo; bed © iStockphoto; family © monkeybusinessimages/Bigstock

Table of Contents

Introduction

Mention the word *grammar* to the tech-savvy multitaskers who inhabit our classrooms, and they might respond, "OMG, are you from the Dark Ages, lady? Get a life!" In the 21st century, how do we teach grammar? To create relevant lessons and improve student achievement, incorporating technology is essential. Marzano and Haystead's (2009) study of interactive whiteboards demonstrates that dropping and dragging activities, uncovering information hidden by graphics, and applauding correct answers resulted in a 31 percentile point gain in student achievement. Moreover, Harrison and Hummel (2010) proved that animations utilized in whiteboard lessons not only do a better job of conveying the content than the static blackboard, but they also help students understand and master abstract concepts. Thus, using technology to teach a concept as abstract as grammar makes sense and positively impacts student learning and achievement.

Our purpose for writing this book is to engage students in meaningful learning that utilizes technology and an instructional model supported by research to teach grammar in the context of writing. The relevance of our approach is underscored in IRA/NCTE standard 6, which emphasizes the importance of applying "knowledge of language structure and language conventions" to writing. As Polette (2008) states, teaching grammar through writing is the most effective way to help students develop their writing skills. We invite you to join us on our journey into teaching grammar in the 21st century.

What's Inside

As the book's title indicates, you will find 15 lessons that tackle hard-to-teach grammar skills. Each lesson includes the following:
- a critical question designed to focus the learning
- a warm-up to motivate students and activate their prior knowledge (Marzano, 2003)
- a step-by-step instructional guide that utilizes modeling (Marzano, 2007)
- guided and independent practice for students (Marzano, 2007)
- a wrap-up to help students summarize their learning (Marzano, 2010)
- a writing connection that connects the grammatical concept to writing, when appropriate.

The SMART Board® is carefully integrated into the instruction in each lesson, and the lessons and reproducible activities are crafted to keep the class active and engaged. They also involve inquiry and discovery learning (Irvin, Meltzer, & Dukes, 2007; Powell & Kalina, 2009; Jensen, 2002; and Stevens-Smith, 2004). Therefore, directions and activities for seated students as well as the student volunteers who are utilizing the interactive whiteboard are important components of each lesson. The teaching time for each lesson varies—some lesson plans, such as "Introduction to Run-On Sentences," may take a few days, while others, such as "Varying Sentence Beginnings," take only a class period.

Based on the diagnostic writing prompts we give our students, the number-one problem they have with conventions is the run-on sentence. Consequently, the first three lessons are devoted to repairing run-on sentences. The first lesson provides the background information students need to be able to identify and correct their errors. The next two lessons target run-ons in compound sentences and the comma splice. To help students apply what they learn to their writing, they correct errors in a paragraph.

In Lessons 4 through 8, students explore vivid verbs in writing, examine helping verbs, change passive voice to active voice, maintain correct verb tense in a piece of writing, and utilize confusing verb pairs correctly.

Because Dorfman and Cappelli (2007) believe that vivid verbs and precise nouns significantly improve students' writing styles, Lessons 9 through 11 explore using proper nouns to improve specificity in writing. In this section, we also focus on spelling plural nouns and using possessive nouns correctly.

The last four lessons investigate prepositions. Students first are introduced to prepositions and prepositional phrases. Then we connect the concept to writing, demonstrating how to use prepositional phrases to add description and to vary sentence beginnings.

How to Incorporate the SMART Board

The attached CD contains 15 SMART Notebook files correlated to the lessons in this book. Each lesson offers step-by-step procedures on how to have students interact with your lesson via the SMART Board. For instance, we have included features, such as the screen shade and cell shade, which allow for material to be covered temporarily. When you are ready to reveal the next portion of the lesson to the students, you can simply touch the cell shade or drag the screen shade to uncover the material. In addition to the shades, we have included some unique methods for students to reveal the answers. Students will make use of the magnifying glass, the eraser tool, the pen tool, the drag-and-drop feature, and many more interactive methods. Instructions on what to do on screen are in the PULL arrows. Simply drag them out to read the directions.

Before students arrive, have your SMART Board ready to go. Load the CD onto your host computer and copy all the files onto your hard drive. This way, you can work off the local files when you're ready to teach a lesson. As with any technology, it is always a good idea to try out the SMART Board lessons on your own first before presenting them to the class.

NOTE: You will need the SMART Notebook software to open the activities on the CD. If you do not have the software, you can go to http://express.smarttech.com to open the Notebook file online or download the free SMART Notebook Express Software onto your computer.

Correlations With the Common Core State Standards

The lessons in this book and on the CD help students meet the following Common Core State Standards.

Language Standards (Conventions of Standard English)

L.4.1, L.5.1, L.6.1, L.7.1, L.8.1 – Demonstrate command of the conventions of standard English grammar and usage when writing or speaking.
- **L.4.1b** Form and use the progressive verb tenses.
- **L.4.1c** Use modal auxiliaries to convey various conditions.
- **L.4.1e** Form and use prepositional phrases.
- **L.4.1f** Produce complete sentences, recognizing and correcting inappropriate fragments and run-ons.
- **L.5.1a** Explain the function of conjunctions, prepositions, and interjections in general and their function in particular sentences.
- **L.5.1b** Form and use the perfect verb tenses.
- **L.5.1c** Use verb tense to convey various times, sequences, states, and conditions.
- **L.5.1d** Recognize and correct inappropriate shifts in verb tense.
- **L.8.1b** Form and use verbs in the active and passive voice.

L.4.2, L.5.2, L.6.2, L.7.2, L.8.2 – Demonstrate command of the conventions of standard English capitalization, punctuation, and spelling when writing.
- **L.4.2c** Use a comma before a coordinating conjunction in a compound sentence.

Source: Common Core State Standards Initiative
http://www.corestandards.org/the-standards/english-language-arts-standards

Lesson 1
Introduction to Run-On Sentences

Critical Question: How can you identify a run-on sentence and correct it in your writing?

You Need:

- Any puppet with a big mouth or a sock puppet
- "1 Run-On Sentences" SMART Notebook file (on CD)
- Class copies of "The Problems With Run-Ons" (page 9)
- Class copies of "How to Fix Run-Ons" (page 10)

Warm-Up: Using any puppet with a big mouth, fire one sentence after another at students. In one breath, have the puppet yammer through a run-on sentence such as this:

> *"Hi I'm Big Mouth Bob, the biggest blabber-mouth in town, so people tell me but I don't believe them because I think they are jealous of me because I'm a happening dude who can spin a tale and entertain folks. Why just yesterday when I was downtown shopping some diamond-studded grandma's pet poodle grabbed hold of my tail with its razor-sharp, itsy-bitsy teeth well I swatted my tail back and forth like a jet propeller but that feisty little furball wouldn't budge."*

After such a dramatic introduction, gasp for breath and ask students: *What grammar and writing problem did I just demonstrate?* (Run-on sentence) Once students have identified the problem, continue on to "What to Do," which outlines the three ways to fix run-ons.

What to Do:

1. Display the SMART Notebook file titled "1 Run-On Sentences" on the interactive whiteboard. Read aloud the question, "What is a run-on sentence?" and ask students what they think. After listening to a few ideas, pull on the runner. Explain to students that there are three common run-on problems, then touch the right arrow on the screen to go to the next page.

2. Distribute copies of "The Problems With Run-Ons" to students. Ask them to take notes on this sheet as they learn about three types of run-ons and how to fix them.

3. Press the "1" button on page 2 of the Notebook file. Invite a student to read the first problem: **Two or more sentences run together without any punctuation.** Have the student read the example run-on sentence as well. Then, ask the class for suggestions on what punctuation they could use to fix the run-on. Touch the right arrow to show students two ways they can fix the run-on sentence. Use the eraser tool on the first example to reveal the period that ends the first sentence and the capitalized letter that begins the second sentence. Use the eraser again on the second example to show the comma and the conjunction *so* that connect both ideas. Have students write the solutions on their sheet under "How to Fix."

4. Touch the right arrow for students to practice what they learned. To reveal the correct solutions, drag the graphics on the left side of the screen to their respective shadows on the right. Then press the home button to navigate back to page 2 of the Notebook file.

5. Touch the "2" button to reveal the second run-on problem: **Two sentences are joined together with a conjunction (and, but, or, so, yet, for, nor), but there is no comma to go with the conjunction.** Call on a volunteer to read the example run-on sentence. Ask: *What is the conjunction in the run-on sentence?* (but) Touch the right arrow to show how to fix the run-on sentence. Explain that the comma always comes before the conjunction, and drag the red comma before *but*. Remind students to fill in the "How to Fix" line on their sheet.

6. Touch the right arrow for more practice fixing run-on sentences. Ask students: *Where should the comma go to fix these run-on sentences?* (Before the word *but*) Call on volunteers to drag the red comma to the appropriate place. Then, press the home button to navigate back to page 2 of the Notebook file.

7. To show the third run-on problem, press the "3" button. Invite a student volunteer to read the third problem: **Two or more sentences are joined with a comma.** Read the sample run-on sentence. Explain to students the difference between this run-on problem and the previous one. In the previous problem, we wanted to emphasize the connection between the two sentences, so we joined them together using a comma and a conjunction. In this example, there is no conjunction, only a comma. This particular problem calls for one of two solutions. Touch the right arrow to show the two ways we can fix this run-on. Explain that the first way is to use a semicolon to show that the two ideas are related. Call on a volunteer to drag the magnifying glass over the first example. The semicolon will appear after the word *college*. The second way to solve the run-on is by using ending punctuation and capitalization. Ask another volunteer to drag the magnifying glass over the second example to find out where the ending punctuation and capital letter go. Remind students to take notes.

8. Touch the right arrow to give students a chance to try out what they've learned. Then press the home button to return to page 2.

Wrap-Up: Touch the "Recap" button to review and assess what students have learned. Call on volunteers to explain what each solution means. Then distribute copies of "How to Fix Run-Ons." Have students work in pairs to complete the cloze passage. When students have finished, touch the "Summary" button on page 2 of the Notebook file so students can check their answers. Use the eraser to reveal the answers.

The Problems With Run-Ons

RUN-ON PROBLEM #1: _____

_____

Example: Mr. Smith was late for dinner he was no longer on Mrs. Smith's good side.

HOW TO FIX:

1. _____

   Mr. Smith was late for dinner__ ___e was no longer on Mrs. Smith's good side.

2. _____

   Mr. Smith was late for dinner__ _____ he was no longer on Mrs. Smith's good side.

RUN-ON PROBLEM #2: _____

_____

Example: Paul knew he had to stick to his diet but that luscious chocolate cake was
          too good to resist.

HOW TO FIX:

_____

   Paul knew he had to stick to his diet__ but that luscious chocolate cake was
   too good to resist.

RUN-ON PROBLEM #3: _____

_____

Example: Mrs. Davis used to play field hockey in college, now she exercises at the gym
          to stay in shape.

HOW TO FIX:

1. _____

   Mrs. Davis used to play field hockey in college__ now she exercises at the gym
   to stay in shape.

2. _____

   Mrs. Davis used to play field hockey in college__ ___ow she exercises at the gym
   to stay in shape.

How to Fix Run-Ons

Directions: Fill in the blanks. Choose from the word bank below.

One way to correct a run-on sentence is to use proper

_____ and _____ punctuation to

create _____ or more sentences.

If a coordinating conjunction, such as _____,

connects two sentences, you MUST put a _____

before the conjunction to avoid a _____ sentence.

You cannot connect two sentences with just a

_____, or you create a run-on sentence.

Instead of using a comma to connect two sentences, add a

_____ if the two sentences are closely related.

WORD BANK

comma	end	semicolon	two
and	capitalization	comma	run-on

Lesson 2

Run-Ons in Compound Sentences

Critical Question: How do you correct run-ons in compound sentences?

You Need:

- "2 Run-ons in Compound Sentences" SMART Notebook file (on CD)
- "Commas for Compound Sentences" (page 13)—Make enough copies on cardstock for pairs of students. Laminate and cut apart the strips, then store each set of strips in a plastic bag.
- Dry-erase markers (for each pair of students)
- Paper towels
- Index cards (one card per student)

Warm-Up: Display the SMART Notebook file titled "2 Run-Ons in Compound Sentences" on the interactive whiteboard. Pull on the runner to review the definition of a compound sentence with students. For a quick review of conjunctions, touch the music player to view the "Conjunction Song" music video. Use this video to teach the class all of the coordinating conjunctions. Have students practice and memorize the song:

And, but, or, so, yet, for, nor,
comma before (repeat)

Explain that a compound sentence could end up being a run-on sentence if proper punctuation is not used.

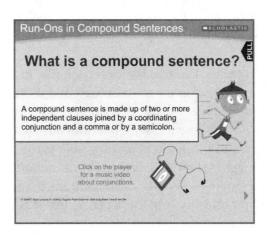

What to Do:

1. Touch the right arrow to go to the next page. Point to the sentence in red and ask students: *Why is this sentence a run-on?* (It is missing a comma.) Explain that using just a conjunction to connect two sentences is not enough. Remind students of Rule #2 from the previous lesson: We need to place a comma before the conjunction. Click on the right arrow to show how to correct the run-on. Guide students to notice that each clause in the sentence can stand alone as a shorter sentence: *The math monster devours math books. He eats calculators, too.* Remind students that a complete sentence contains a subject and a verb and expresses a complete thought.

2. Touch the right arrow to go to the next page. Call on a volunteer to read the top sentence. Ask: *Do we need a comma before the word* and *in this sentence?* (No) *How can you tell when to put a comma before a conjunction?* Using the sample sentence, model the Index Finger Test: Drag the hand icon and place it on top of *and* to check if there is a complete sentence on either side of the conjunction. Read the first part of the sentence aloud and ask students if it can stand alone as a sentence. *(Yes)* Read the second part aloud and ask if it is a sentence. *(No; there is no subject, so it is not a complete sentence.)* Explain that because the second part cannot stand alone, a comma is not needed before the word *and* in this sentence.

3. On pages 4 to 8 of the Notebook file, invite students to come to the board and do the Index Finger Test to determine if a comma is needed in each sentence. Encourage them to think aloud as they take turns dragging the hand over the conjunction. If a comma is needed, have them move the hand and use a SMART pen to insert a comma in the correct place.

4. Go to page 9 of the Notebook file and ask students to stand beside their desks. Tell them that you will show them one sentence at a time, and they should decide whether the sentence is a run-on or a complete sentence. If the sentence is a run-on, they should run in place; if it is a complete sentence, they should create a circle with their hands. (To prevent piggybacking, use a signal clue, such as "Show me now," after students have had time to think about their answers.) Then touch the star to check their answers. If the star spins, then the sentence is a complete sentence; if the star fades out, that indicates a run-on.

5. Pair up students and give each pair a plastic bag containing the "Commas for Compound Sentences" strips, a dry-erase marker, and a paper towel. Have partners take turns doing the Index Finger Test and inserting commas on the strips when necessary. (Answers are on page 10 of the Notebook file.) To clean up, have students wipe the strips clean with a paper towel and return the strips to the bag.

Wrap-Up: Hand each student an index card. Ask students to write either a run-on compound sentence or a complete sentence containing a comma and conjunction. Then have partners exchange index cards and determine if the sentence is complete or a run-on. If it is a run-on, have students correct it. Collect the index cards to monitor student progress.

Commas for Compound Sentences

You must eat your brussel sprouts or you can't go to the movies.

Molly whines about her freezing feet but won't use a blanket.

Floss after eating corn on the cob or your teeth will be mellow yellow.

Sheldon better return my book or he is in big trouble!

The dentist couldn't locate the incisor but he pulled something out anyway.

I'm happy I went to the party for I danced with the girl of my dreams.

Don't forget your tickets to the concert or you will be singing the blues outside.

Clip your toenails for they will poke right through your socks.

I knew you were talented but didn't think you could pull spaghetti noodles through your nose!

Horace trusted his mom but then she raided his candy jar and ate all of the peanut butter cups.

Lesson 3
Comma Splices

Critical Question: How do you identify and correct comma splices?

What is a comma splice?

When you connect two complete sentences with a comma, you create a comma splice.

You Need:

• "3 Comma Splices" SMART Notebook file (on CD)

• Class copies of "Comma Splice, Not So Nice" (page 15)

• Class copies of "Hot Holiday!" (page 16)

• Notebook paper

Warm-Up: Display the SMART Notebook file titled "3 Comma Splices" on the interactive whiteboard. Pull on the runner for a definition of a comma splice. Press the right arrow to go to page 2. Read aloud the rule at the top of the screen. Then, covering the comma in the example below the rule, show how the comma connects two complete sentences. Explain to students that the comma creates another type of run-on called a comma splice. Ask: *What are some ways we can fix this grammar mistake?*

What to Do:

1. Click on the child to see three ways to correct the comma splice. Touch each correction box, one at a time, to uncover each solution.

   • **Replace the comma with a period and capitalize to start a new sentence.**

   • **Replace the comma with a semicolon.**

   • **Add an appropriate conjunction after the comma.**

2. Go to the next page of the Notebook file. Invite a student to come to the SMART Board to use the Index Finger Test (see page 11) to determine whether the first sentence is a comma splice or a complete sentence. Have the student touch the star to check his or her answer. A spinning star means it is a

complete sentence, while a disappearing star indicates it is a run-on.

3. On pages 5 and 6 of the Notebook file, students can fix the two run-on sentences from the previous activity. Ask volunteers to fix the comma splices by dragging the appropriate red punctuation mark into the space between sentences. Then challenge students to explain the differences among the three types of corrections.

4. Distribute copies of "Comma Splice, Not So Nice" to students for additional practice. Answers are on pages 7 and 8 of the Notebook file.

Wrap-Up: Have students take a piece of notebook paper and write one complete sentence and one comma splice. Remind students to mix up their examples. After they have finished writing, ask them to exchange papers with a partner. Instruct students to put a star next to the complete sentence and to fix the comma splice.

A Writing Connection!

To help students become effective proofreaders, distribute copies of "Hot Holiday!" Display page 9 of the Notebook file. Have students work in pairs and take turns reading each sentence aloud to listen for the run-ons. Instruct students to draw brackets [ ] around the run-ons and to use proper proofreading symbols to correct them. Remind students to use the Index Finger Test when they come across a conjunction or a comma. Touch the "Answers" button on the screen so students can check their work.

Comma Splice, Not So Nice

Directions: Use the Index Finger Test to determine whether the following sentences are comma splices or complete sentences. Put a star next to the complete sentences and correct the comma splices.

1. Those three blind mice just ran off with the farmer's cheese, he came running after them and sneezed.

2. Humpty Dumpty sat on the wall, I wonder what caused that great big fall.

3. Little Miss Muffet sat on a tuffet, eating her burgers and fries.

4. There was an old lady who lived on a flip-flop, without any children, she took up hip-hop.

5. Old Mother Hubbard went to her cupboard, lots of carbohydrates she did discover.

6. Little Bo Peep lost her sheep, she hopped on her motorcycle to find them.

7. Old McDonald had a farm with a cow, duck, pig, horse, and chicken, of course.

8. When the cow jumped over the moon, Diddle Diddle broke his little fiddle.

9. The Muffin Man, who lives on Drury Lane, brought me breakfast this morning.

10. Peter Piper picked a peck of packaged pencils, how many pecks of packaged pencils did Peter Piper pick?

Name: _____ Date: _____

Hot Holiday!

Directions: Use the following proofreading symbols to identify and fix the run-ons in the student paragraph below.

Proofreading Symbols

Welcome to Hotlantic, where your dreams of no water come true this place is as hot as melted volcanic rock. Watch out for the hot rock falling from the ceiling for it drips down like smooth, creamy whipped cream. You can take a blistering walk into town and get some fresh lava bread with pockets of molten butter. Don't forget to grab a cup of steaming lava cream, which can give you a hot start to your day! If you feel the need to cool down, head down Igneous Avenue and you will find the little store with the red awning. There you will discover their specialty, "The Frozen Flare." It's a scrumptious concoction of frozen, icy, slushy, soft rock. Look around, you will see many weird animals. There are huge creatures with smooth scales and horns of all sizes popping out of their heads. Keep your eyes out for dragons they may swoop down and grab you with their razor-sharp claws. I hope you have a smokin' day!

Lesson 4
Action Verbs

Critical Question: How can action verbs improve writing?

You Need:

- "4 Action Verbs" SMART Notebook file (on CD)

- "Action Verbs in a Basket" (page 19)—Copy on cardstock, laminate, and cut apart. Place the cards facedown in a basket.

- Chart paper

- Markers

- Notebook paper

- A picture book that features vivid verbs, such as *Sweet Tooth* by Margie Palatini (Simon & Schuster, 2004)

- Class copies of "My Life As a _____" (page 20)

- Class copies of "Vivid Verbs Rubric" (page 22)

Warm-Up: Display the SMART Notebook file titled "4 Action Verbs" on the interactive whiteboard. Read aloud the sentence on the screen: *The red dragon WALKED down the street.* Explain to students that the verb *walked* is not a vivid verb. Tell students they are going to act out vivid verbs to replace this trite verb. Call on a volunteer to draw a vivid verb from the basket and begin a game of verb charades. Have the student act out the verb on the card and challenge the class to guess this more-powerful verb choice. After a few guesses, touch the right arrow to display the list of verbs.

Touch the right arrow to display the sentence, *"I love you," SAID the red dragon.* Divide the class into groups of four and provide each group with a piece of chart paper. Direct students to brainstorm a list of vivid verbs to replace the overused verb *said*. After several minutes, ask the class to

The red dragon WALKED down the street.

Can you think of a more vivid verb to replace the word WALKED?

sit in a circle on the floor. Display the chart with the most verbs on it. Call on student volunteers to take turns picking a verb from the list and using voice intonation to express the verb's meaning. For example, if the verb is *bellowed*, the student reads, "I love you" in a loud, angry voice. If the verb is *whispered*, the student says, "I love you" in a soft, quiet voice. Continue until all the verbs have been acted out.

What to Do:

1. Go to page 4 of the Notebook file. Read aloud the two sentences to reinforce the idea that vivid verbs create a clear, distinct picture in the mind, unlike the trite "boo-hisser."

2. Touch the right arrow on the screen. Read each sentence aloud, noting that the red verb is a boo-hisser. Call on a volunteer to touch the red word in the first sentence (the word will fade away) and to use the SMART pen to replace it with a more vivid verb. While the student writes his or her choice on the board, encourage other students to work in pairs to discuss alternate choices for the underlined verb. Repeat with the other two sentences.

3. Touch the right arrow on the screen to display the picture on the next page. Challenge students to generate their own list of applicable vivid verbs that describe the possible actions in the photograph. Encourage students to think beyond the photo to vivid verbs that can describe "potential" actions of the objects in the picture. For example, if the photo shows

cars speeding down the road, the verbs *crash*, *skid*, or *spin* could be associated with this action. Continue this process for the next three pages of the Notebook file.

4. Consider having students choose verbs from their list to add to a "Vivid Verb Wall." Encourage them to type or write the verbs in colorful, large, fancy fonts.

Wrap-Up: In their journals, have students write a paragraph to answer this lesson's critical question.

A Writing Connection!

To help students become effective writers, ask them to write a narrative that incorporates vivid verbs. Read aloud a story that uses vivid verbs, such as *Sweet Tooth* by Margie Palatini. As students listen, have them write down some of the vivid verbs they hear. Afterwards, invite students to share some of their verbs with a partner or generate a class list of verbs on chart paper.

Next, distribute copies of "My Life as a _____" as well as the "Vivid Verbs Rubric" to students. Explain that, like Palatini, they are going to write a narrative about a day in the life of a body part, using vivid verbs, a distinct voice, and the body part's point of view. They will use the "My Life is a _____" worksheet to help them generate ideas for their writing. Encourage students to strive for ten vivid verbs and to underline them in their writing. Carefully review the rubric to let students know your expectations. Continue to guide students through the rest of the writing process for this narrative.

Action Verbs in a Basket

strutted	stumbled
waddled	strolled
staggered	pranced
be-bopped	tiptoed
plodded	pirouetted

My Life as a _____
(name of body part)

elbow, forehead, shoulder, knee, toe, finger, hair,

Purpose of Your Narrative: Tell a story about a typical day in the life of a body part from that part's point of view.

Brainstorming: Before writing, visualize a day in the body part's life. Imagine. Become the body part. Use your mind as a movie camera and picture everything that is happening to you and around you. Think of at least ten vivid verbs that might be associated with that body part.

1. What are you? _____
(name the body part)

2. Briefly describe where you are located on the body: _____

_____

3. Choose at least three of the five senses to describe yourself. Onomatopoeia anyone?

I like _____   I like _____

I like _____   I like _____

I like _____

4. Write an attention-grabbing topic sentence that draws the reader into your life: _____

_____

_____
(continued)

eyebrow, nail, tonsils, cheeks, throat, thigh, brain,

lungs, hand, eyelashes, lips, foot, armpit, voice box, knuckles, heart,

eyes, hip, shin, wrist, biceps, neck, back, ankle, belly button, tongue,

elbow, forehead, shoulder, knee, toe, finger, hair,

5. How do you feel? List three or four of your strongest emotions.

1. _____   3. _____

2. _____   4. _____

6. List three or four interesting or humorous events that occur during a typical day in your life.

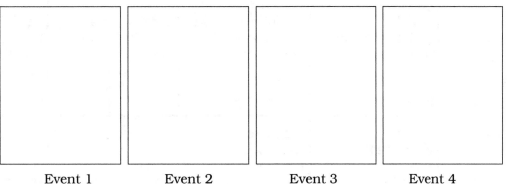

| Event 1 | Event 2 | Event 3 | Event 4 |

7. What do people say to you? _____

_____

_____

8. What are some things you would like to say to your owner?

_____

_____

_____

9. How will your story end? _____

_____

_____

eyebrow, nail, tonsils, cheeks, throat, thigh, brain,

lungs, hand, eyelashes, lips, foot, armpit, voice box, knuckles, heart,

eyes, hip, shin, wrist, biceps, neck, back, ankle, belly button, tongue,

Vivid Verbs Rubric

Criteria for Evaluation	Advanced 4	Proficient 3	Basic 2	Below Basic 1
Focus ____ (score)	The narrative zeroes in on a typical day in the life of the body part.	The narrative stays on topic most of the time.	The narrative sometimes stays on topic.	The narrative frequently strays from the topic or is off topic.
Organization ____ (score)	The narrative contains an attention-grabbing opening, distinct middle, satisfying ending, and excellent transitions.	The narrative contains a beginning, middle, end, and smooth transitions.	The beginning, middle, or end is missing; the narrative lacks continuity and/or needs more transition words.	No clear beginning, middle, or end is present; few, if any, transition words appear.
Content ____ (score)	The narrative vividly describes at least three events in the body part's life and includes numerous details and specifics.	The narrative describes at least three events in the body part's life and includes some details and specifics.	The narrative somewhat describes two or three events in the body part's life and/or has some details and specifics.	The narrative does not adequately describe the events in the body part's life and/or lacks details and specifics.
Usage ____ (score)	Almost no errors in grammar, mechanics, or spelling appear.	Some errors in grammar, mechanics, or spelling appear.	Many errors in grammar, mechanics, or spelling appear.	So many errors in grammar, mechanics, or spelling appear that the meaning is affected.
Style ____ (score)	All ten vivid verbs are underlined, and the voice is completely consistent.	The narrative contains ten vivid verbs; however, a few are incorrectly identified. The tone is usually consistent.	The narrative contains at least eight correctly identified vivid verbs and/or the tone is somewhat consistent.	The narrative contains seven or fewer vivid verbs that may or may not be correctly identified. The tone is not consistent.

Total Score: _____/20

Comments: _____

_____

Lesson 5
Helping Verbs

Critical Question: How are helping verbs useful in writing?

You Need:

- "5 Helping Verbs" SMART Notebook file (on CD)
- Class copies of "The Helping Verbs Song" (page 24)
- Class copies of "Frosty, the Starving Snowman" (page 25)
- 2 different-colored highlighters (for each student)

Warm-Up: Display the SMART Notebook file titled "5 Helping Verbs" on the interactive whiteboard. Press the jingle bells to play a music video of "The Helping Verbs Song." Have students sing along to the tune of "Jingle Bells," so they can memorize the helping verbs.

What to Do:

1. Display page 2 of the Notebook file and ask students: *What do you think is missing in each of these sentences?* (Helping verbs) Explain that, as its name suggests, a helping verb helps the main verb in a sentence. Some helping verbs give a sense of when an action is happening, while others add a particular tone or mood. Note how the helping verb usually comes before the main verb. Call on a volunteer to read aloud the first sentence and guess what helping verb is missing. Then have the student come up to the board and use the eraser tool on the blank line to check his or her answer. Repeat with the other two sentences.

2. Touch the right arrow on the screen to go to the next page. Read aloud the definition of a *verb phrase*. Then ask students to call out the verb phrase in the sample

sentence. (*was sledding*) Ask: *Which word is the helping verb?* (was) Use the SMART pen to highlight the word *was* in yellow. Ask: *Which is the main verb?* (sledding) Highlight the word *sledding* in green.

3. Explain that some verb phrases have more than one helping verb. Touch the right arrow to show an example. Call on a student volunteer to come to the board and highlight the two helping verbs in yellow (*had been*) and the main verb in green (*daydreaming*).

4. Distribute copies of "Frosty, the Starving Snowman" to students. Ask them to look for the verb phrase in each sentence. Share this strategy for finding the verb phrase: *Ask yourselves, "What can I do in this sentence?" and "What helping verbs do I know?"* When students have completed their worksheets, display page 5 of the Notebook file for a replica of the activity. Call on volunteers to come to the board and model the strategy before underlining the verb phrases with the SMART pen. (The sentences continues on page 6.) Touch "Answers" to check students' responses.

Wrap-Up: Go to page 9 of the Notebook file for a sorting activity. Invite volunteers to come to the board one at a time and drag out a word card from the Verbs Box. Have them decide if the word is a helping verb or a main verb and place it in the correct column. In the meantime, distribute two different colored highlighters to seated students and have them highlight the helping verbs on their "Frosty" reproducible in one color and the main verbs in another color. Touch "Answers" when students are finished.

The Helping Verbs Song

(to the tune of "Jingle Bells")

DO DOES DID

HAVE HAS HAD

MAY MIGHT MUST

WOULD COULD SHOULD

WILL SHALL CAN

These are helping verbs!

AM IS ARE

WAS WERE

BE BEING BEEN

These verbs join together

with other verbs!

Frosty, the Starving Snowman

Directions: Underline the verb phrases in the sentences below. Highlight the helping verb in one color and the main verb in another color.

1. Frosty was thinking about food.

2. The hungry snowman did eat his carrot nose.

3. Uh-oh, he might swallow the buttons next.

4. The happy, jolly soul will be wishing for some antacid.

5. That poor fellow might burst!

6. He should have considered the consequences.

7. Ouch! What goes in must come out!

8. He may change his mind in the future.

9. Frosty could have avoided his abdominal pain.

10. Hey, maybe he should have been called the "abdominal" snowman!

Active Voice

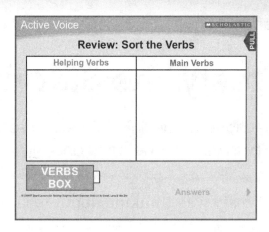

Critical Question: How can replacing helping verbs with action verbs improve writing?

You Need:

• "6 Active Voice" SMART Notebook file (on CD)

• Class copies of "Active Class Action" (page 27)

• Class copies of "Tricky Slick" (page 28)

Warm-Up: Review helping verbs with students. Display the SMART Notebook file titled "6 Active Voice" on the interactive whiteboard. Call on student volunteers to come to the board to drag the word cards from the Verbs Box and sort the helping verbs from the main verbs. Touch "Answers" when all the cards have been sorted. Ask: *What do helping verbs do?* (They help the main verb by giving a sense of when the action is happening or by giving it a particular tone or mood.) Then suggest to students that relying too heavily on helping verbs can weaken the impact of their writing.

What to Do:

1. Explain to students that helping verbs sometimes prevent good writing. Go to page 3 of the Notebook file and read the sentence on the screen. Touch above the red words to reveal what is wrong with the sentence. Explain that the helping verb *were* creates a sentence that uses the passive voice. Show how the subject (the banker's shoes) *receives* the verb's action instead of *doing* the action. Point out that the mischievous dragon is actually the one filling the shoes with the shaving cream and should be the subject in the sentence.

2. Touch the right arrow on the screen to go to the next page. Tell students that to give the sentence an active voice, they need to eliminate the helping verb *were*, then rearrange and/or eliminate some words. Call on a student volunteer to come to the board and demonstrate this strategy. Encourage the student to move around the phrases to create an active voice. *(The mischievous dragon filled the banker's shoes with shaving cream.)*

3. Next, distribute copies of "Active Class Action" to students. Display page 5 of the Notebook file on the interactive whiteboard. Use the first sentence to model the strategy for changing passive voice to active voice. First, drag the helping verb out of the sentence and into the trash. Then rearrange the words to create a sentence using the active voice. Have students copy the changes on their reproducible. Then invite volunteers to use the strategy to fix the other sentences on the board, while seated students work on their sheet. Touch "Answers" to check students' responses.

Wrap-Up: Distribute copies of "Tricky Slick" to students. As a whole class, use the strategy for changing passive voice to active voice to correct the first sentence. Then have students complete the rest of the paragraph for independent practice. Display page 7 of the Notebook file on the interactive whiteboard for a possible answer. Engage students in a discussion of the lesson's critical question.

Active Class Action

Directions: Change the sentences from passive to active voice. First, cross out the helping verb(s). Then, rearrange and/or eliminate words to create a sentence with active voice.

1. The shy student's locker is stuffed with phony love notes by the naughty dragon.

_____

_____.

2. In the science lab, frogs are removed from their cages by the giggling prankster.

_____

_____.

3. Moldy liverwurst sandwiches were inserted into the student's lunch box by the flying comedian.

_____

_____.

4. During English class, a whoopie cushion was placed on the teacher's seat by the fiery imp.

_____

_____.

5. Consequently, the students were sent to detention by the furious teacher.

_____

_____.

Tricky Slick

Directions: Rewrite the following paragraph to give it an active voice.

Perfectly horrific tricks were played on the entire school by Slick, the spunky teenage dragon. Mr. Sharp, the well-dressed principal, was hypnotized by the prankster and came to school wearing his pants upside down and his shirt backwards. Next, the phone numbers from everyone's cell phones were removed by him. Over the loudspeaker, an announcement was made by Slick that all students were required to wear the turkey feathers from their art projects to gym class. Consequently, jumping jacks appeared to be done by "gobblers" instead of students. Because of the feathers stuck to his tail, the jokester was caught by the gym teacher. The teacher was secretly texted by Slick on his way to detention. The message that was written by him said, "Detention has been canceled for today."

_____

_____

_____

_____

_____

_____

_____

_____

_____

_____

Lesson 7
Verb Tenses

Critical Question: How is the correct tense maintained in a piece of writing?

You Need:

- "What Tense Is It?" (pages 31–32) — Photocopy onto cardstock, then laminate and cut apart the sentence strips. Put the strips in a plastic bag or container.
- Three signs labeled "Past," "Present," and "Future"
- "7 Verb Tenses" SMART Notebook file (on CD)
- Class copies of "Verb Tense Notes" (page 33) — Cut into halves.
- Red and blue index cards
- Notebook paper or journals
- Class copies of "Kayaking Catastrophe (I)" (page 34) — for advanced learners
- Class copies of "Kayaking Catastrophe (II)" (page 35) — for students who need support

Warm-Up: Prepare three signs labeled "Past," "Present," and "Future." Post them in three different areas of the classroom. To activate students' prior knowledge of verbs, give each student a sentence strip from "What Tense Is It?" as he or she walks in the door. Have each student read the sentence strip and stand next to the appropriate sign based on the verb tense in the sentence. Invite students at each location to compare their verbs with one another and explain why their verb is that specific tense. Have each group appoint a reporter to share their thoughts with the rest of the class. Then ask students to return to their seats.

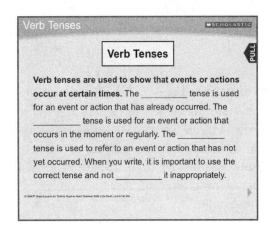

Verb Tenses

Verb tenses are used to show that events or actions occur at certain times. The _____ tense is used for an event or action that has already occurred. The _____ tense is used for an event or action that occurs in the moment or regularly. The _____ tense is used to refer to an event or action that has not yet occurred. When you write, it is important to use the correct tense and not _____ it inappropriately.

What to Do:

1. Display the SMART Notebook file titled "7 Verb Tenses" on the interactive whiteboard. Distribute copies of "Verb Tense Notes" to students. Have students work in pairs to identify the correct verb tenses and fill in the blanks. Then touch the blanks on the board to reveal the answers. When you reach the last sentence, explain to students that correct verb tense must be maintained throughout a piece of writing. Point out the word *not* (written in red letters) to emphasize that they should not switch tenses in their writing, unless it is appropriate.

2. Distribute one red and one blue index card to each student. Touch the right arrow on the screen to go to the next page. Call on a volunteer to read the first sentence aloud. Instruct other students to decide if the sentence uses the correct verb tense. If they think the verb tense is correct, students should hold up their blue index card; if incorrect, they should hold up the red card. At your signal (e.g., when you say, "Show me"), have students reveal their answers at the same time. Have the volunteer touch the blue or red box, depending on his or her answer. The box will reveal if he or she is correct. Ask the student to justify his or her answer and correct the verb tense, if necessary. Repeat the process for each sentence on pages 2 to 6 of the Notebook file, calling on a different volunteer each time.

Wrap-Up: Go to page 7 of the Notebook file to introduce the "3-2-1 Review" strategy to students. Pull down the screen shade one step at a time. Using this strategy, have students summarize their understanding of verb tense on a piece of notebook paper or in their journals.

A Writing Connection!

To reinforce the concept of maintaining correct verb tense in a piece of writing, distribute copies of "Kayaking Catastrophe (I)" to students. (For students who struggle in this area, use "Kayaking Catastrophe (II).") Have students work individually or with a partner to identify and correct the ten verb tense errors in the passage. When everyone has finished, display page 8 of the Notebook file (for version I) on the interactive whiteboard. (Display page 9 for version II.) To reveal the answers, pull out the kayak on the upper right-hand corner to cover its shadow on the upper left-hand corner. Discuss any questions or problems students might have with the activity.

What Tense Is It?

In field hockey, a forward <u>dribbles</u> the ball.

Last Sunday at the soccer tournament, our team <u>won</u>!

<u>Will</u> you <u>go</u> to the ice hockey game on Saturday?

A pitcher <u>has</u> a strong arm.

Last Friday night, the quarterback <u>threw</u> a 70-yard pass.

Next year, I <u>will join</u> the fast-pitch softball team.

The ball <u>swishes</u> into the basket for a three-pointer!

During the volleyball game, the spiker <u>slammed</u> the ball.

At this afternoon's swim practice, the coach <u>will provide</u> team-winning advice.

After school every day, Chad <u>performs</u> ollies.

On the 9th green, my dad <u>bogeyed</u> the hole.

My new racket <u>shall improve</u> my backswing!

On the slopes, I <u>ramp</u> the moguls with ease.

My brother <u>crossed</u> the wake at 30 miles per hour on his jet ski.

Sweaty fingers <u>will stick</u> in bowling ball holes.

(continued)

What Tense Is It?

Your teacher <u>soars</u> gracefully when she <u>skydives</u>.

The gymnast <u>landed</u> a perfect score for her routine.

In the summer, we <u>will cruise</u> the hills on our dirt bikes.

On the stage, the young ballerina <u>pirouettes</u>.

The cheerleading squad <u>earned</u> a national award.

Our family <u>will travel</u> to a fly-fishing competition in Canada.

On the cruise, we <u>snorkel</u> daily.

The sumo wrestler <u>flipped</u> his opponent.

During the archery competition, the hunter <u>will hit</u> his mark.

The hiker <u>splashes</u> his face with cold water from the stream.

Before the marathon, the runner <u>stretched</u> her calf muscles.

At the party, the teenagers <u>will play</u> badminton.

We usually <u>surf</u> until the sun <u>goes</u> down.

The yacht owner <u>hoisted</u> his sails at dawn.

At the backyard BBQ, the kids <u>will toss</u> horseshoes.

Verb Tense Notes

Name: _____ Date: _____

Verb tenses are used to show that events or actions occur at certain times. The _____ tense is used for an event or action that has already occurred. The _____ tense is used for an event or action that occurs in the moment or regularly. The _____ tense is used to refer to an event or action that has not yet occurred. When you write, it is important to use the correct tense and not _____ it inappropriately.

Name: _____ Date: _____

Verb tenses are used to show that events or actions occur at certain times. The _____ tense is used for an event or action that has already occurred. The _____ tense is used for an event or action that occurs in the moment or regularly. The _____ tense is used to refer to an event or action that has not yet occurred. When you write, it is important to use the correct tense and not _____ it inappropriately.

Kayaking Catastrophe (I)

Directions: Read the following paragraph. Underline the ten verb tense errors. Above each error, write the correct verb tense.

Was kayaking really the perfect sport for all ages? If you ask my friend Tammy, she will retort, "Usually, but not if you are with my friend Susan! The last kayaking adventure we shared, Susan stands up and tipped the kayak at the edge of the dock. Then she lands headfirst in the shallow water and surfaces with seaweed covering her entire body! Worse yet, she smells like a dead fish, and we have to drive forty miles to return home. Needless to say, I rolled down all of the windows, but that still does not help much. The stench was horrendous!" So, even though kayaking was supposed to be a low-impact sport that people of all ages can enjoy, consider taking a lesson or two to be safe. Whatever you did, always remember to wear a life vest because you never knew just how uncoordinated you or your partner might be!

Kayaking Catastrophe (II)

Directions: Read the following paragraph. Underline the ten verb tense errors. Above each error, write the correct verb tense.

The last kayaking adventure Susan and I shared turns out to be quite memorable! My very uncoordinated friend earned the name "Susan, the Seaweed Monster." It all begins when we arrived at the lake. Susan stands up and tipped the kayak at the edge of the dock. Then she lands headfirst in the shallow water and surfaces with seaweed covering her entire body! Worse yet, she smells like a dead fish, and we have to drive forty miles to return home. Needless to say, I rolled down all of the windows, but that still does not help much. The stench was horrendous! Ha, and I thought kayaking was supposed to be a low-impact sport anyone could enjoy. I ask Susan to consider taking a kayaking safety course before our next trip. As she pulls strands of seaweed from her hair, she sputtered, "Good idea!"

Lesson 8

Confusing Verb Pairs

Critical Question: How do you choose the correct form of confusing verb pairs?

You Need:

• "8 Confusing Verb Pairs" SMART Notebook file (on CD)

• "Sorting Confusing Verb Pairs" (page 38) — Make enough copies on cardstock for pairs of students. Laminate and cut apart the cards (including the category headers), then store each set of cards in a plastic bag.

• Notebook paper

• Class copies of "Setting Verb Pairs Straight" (page 39)

• Class copies of "Taking Flight" (page 40)

Warm-Up: Display the SMART Notebook file titled "8 Confusing Verb Pairs" on the interactive whiteboard. Review the present, past, and past participle forms of regular verbs by pressing on each of the gray boxes. Ask students: *What differences do you see among the three forms?* (The present verbs is the same as the base form, while the past tense and past participle end in –ed.) Point out that when used in a verb phrase, the past participle usually includes the verb *has* or *have*. NOTE: The past participle is used to form the perfect tenses. Touch the right arrow to go to the next page and repeat the process to examine conjugations for irregular verbs.

Pair up students and distribute the bags containing the "Sorting Confusing Verb Pairs" cards. Explain to students that the bag contains four category headings: "Base Form," "Present," "Past," and "Past Participle" (black cards with white type). The other cards feature verb forms for *sit, set, rise, raise, lie,* and *lay*. Have students sort the verb cards into the correct category. To guide students through this activity, display page 3 of the Notebook

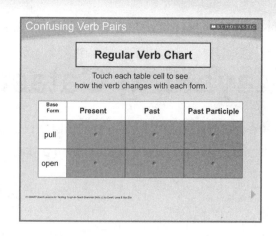

file to model the categories. When students have finished the activity, touch the "Answers" button to reveal the answer key.

What to Do:

1. Tell students: *Some pairs of verbs are so similar to each other that their meanings are often confused. In this lesson, we will discuss confusing verb pairs that are often used incorrectly in speaking and writing.* Distribute copies of "Setting Verb Pairs Straight" to students and ask them to take notes on the sheet.

2. Display page 5 of the Notebook file and read aloud the definitions of the verbs *sit* and *set*. Then touch the gray boxes to reveal the correct conjugations for these verbs. As you review the verb chart, remind students to take notes on their reproducible page.

3. Touch the right arrow on the screen to provide practice using *sit/set* correctly. Call a student volunteer to the board to touch one of the verb choices provided in the first sentence, while seated students record their answer on their reproducible. If the volunteer selects the correct verb, the verb will spin; otherwise, the verb will fade away. Seated students can then check their answers. Call on other volunteers to practice with the remaining sentences.

4. Repeat steps 2 and 3 for the verbs *rise/raise* and *lie/lay* on pages 7–10 of the Notebook file.

5. For independent practice, distribute copies of "Taking Flight" to students. After they have finished, display page 11 of the Notebook file so students can check

their answers. Drag the plane on the upper right hand corner of the page to its shadow on the left.

Wrap-Up: Display page 12 of the Notebook file on the interactive whiteboard. Call on student volunteers to come to the board and drag each verb to its corresponding picture. Ask each volunteer to justify his or her match based on the definition of the verb. Have seated students show a "thumbs up" if they agree or a "thumbs down" if they disagree, providing explanations when necessary.

Next, have students count off numbers from one through six. Click the "Answers" button to reveal the numbered pictures. On notebook paper, have students write three different sentences using their numbered verb. One sentence should be in the present tense, one in the past tense, and one in the perfect tense using the past participle.

A Writing Connection!

Display page 14 of the Notebook file on the interactive whiteboard. Ask a student volunteer to read aloud the poem, pressing on each red verb along the way. Then, challenge students to write a short poem or paragraph, using each of the confusing verb pairs correctly. Invite students to share their work with the rest of the class.

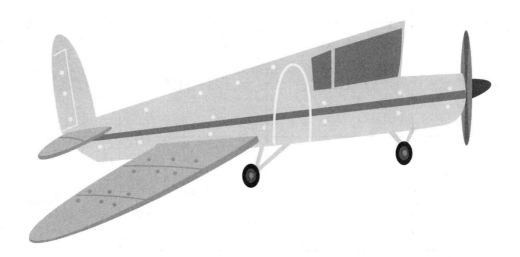

Sorting Confusing Verb Pairs

Base Form	Present	Past	Past Participle
sit	sit	sat	sat
set	set	set	set
rise	rise	rose	risen
raise	raise	raised	raised
lie	lie	lay	lain
lay	lay	laid	laid

Setting Verb Pairs Straight

Directions: Complete the charts. Then circle the correct verb in each sentence.

Base Form	Present	Past	Past Participle
sit – to be seated or to rest			
set – to put (something) in a place			

1. At the picnic, we **(sit / set)** the food on the table.
2. Then we **(sat / set)** on the chairs near the pool.
3. While we were **(sitting / setting)** there, we heard a scream.
4. An enormous wasp had **(sat / set)** itself down on top of the potato salad!
5. Fortunately, the insect did not **(sit /set)** down on one of us.

Base Form	Present	Past	Past Participle
rise – to go up or to get up			
raise – to lift (something) up			

1. After the moon has **(risen / raised)** over the park, the band prepares to play.
2. They are **(rising / raising)** their instruments to tune them.
3. As the musicians start playing their first song, the excited crowd **(rises / raises)** to its feet.
4. Everyone **(rose / raised)** their hands and clapped.
5. Throughout the night, the noise **(rose / raised)** to the sky.

Base Form	Present	Past	Past Participle
lie – to recline			
lay – to put or place (something) down			

1. Before she went to bed, the runner had already carefully **(lain / laid)** her uniform inside her gym bag.
2. Her track shoes **(lay / laid)** at the bottom of the bag.
3. Her cat was already **(lying / laying)** on her pillow.
4. As she **(lay / laid)** in bed, the runner thought about her race the next day.
5. She promised herself she would **(lie / lay)** everything on the line and win.

Taking Flight

Directions: Underline or highlight the <u>ten</u> verbs that are used incorrectly in the following paragraph. Then change them to the correct verb form.

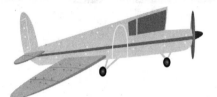

Taking Flight

As the tiny plane raised skyward, my heart began to thump. Below us lay cornfields and cow-studded pastures. The cold, metal bench on which I set made me shiver. When we reached an altitude of 13,000 feet, my stomach felt as if it were raising into my chest, and I began to shake. Slowly I raised from the bench, tightened my harness, and lowered my goggles. I froze as I stared at the minute homes, people, and animals that laid so far below me.

"Jump now!" the instructor commanded. In the air, I arched my back and rose my hands parallel to my body as I soared through the sky like a wingless bird. The parachute set safely on my back. I jerked as I pulled the cord and sat my hands inside the straps controlling the chute. Gently I floated above the earth, amazed by the beauty that was laying beneath me. Before I knew it, we were landing. With knees bent, I sat my feet firmly on the ground.

Lesson 9

Common and Proper Nouns

Critical Question: How can proper nouns make writing more specific and interesting?

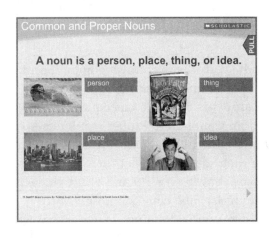

You Need:

- "9 Common and Proper Nouns" SMART Notebook file (on CD)

- Class copies of "The Great Noun Race" (page 43)

- "From Common to Proper" (page 44) — Make enough copies on cardstock for pairs of students. Laminate and cut apart the strips, then store each set of strips in a plastic bag.

- Slips of paper or index cards

Warm-Up: Display the SMART Notebook file titled "9 Common and Proper Nouns" on the interactive whiteboard. Review the definition of *noun* with students, then ask them to examine the pictures and words. The green box next to each picture shows which definition of noun the picture portrays. Touch the green box to see an example of a common noun. Then touch the box again to see an example of a proper noun. Ask students: *What's the difference between the two nouns that you see?* Guide students to define a proper noun as a particular person, place, or thing, which is also capitalized. A common noun, on the other hand, does not name a particular person, place, thing, or idea and is not capitalized. Pair up students and ask each pair to generate a list of more examples of common and proper nouns related to people. Repeat for places, things, and ideas.

What to Do:

1. Touch the right arrow to go to the next page of the Notebook file. Invite a student volunteer to come to the board, read a noun on a balloon, and state whether it is common or proper. Have the volunteer touch the balloon to reveal the correct answer. If the word is a common noun, ask the volunteer to call on another student to provide an example of a proper noun. If the word is a proper noun, have the volunteer select a student to provide an example of a common noun. Repeat this process with other volunteers until all balloons have flown away.

2. Distribute copies of "The Great Noun Race" to students and display page 3 of the Notebook file on the board. Pair students and have them work collaboratively to identify all the common and proper nouns in the paragraph. (Remind students not to include pronouns, such as *they* or *he*.) Tell students that the first pair to correctly find all the nouns wins. To keep track of the order in which pairs finish, give each pair a number on an index card or piece of paper as they finish. When everyone has finished, drag the shopping bag on the upper right-hand corner of the screen to its shadow on the left to reveal the correct answers. Announce as winners the pair who found all the correct answers (or the highest number correct) and finished earliest.

3. To help students connect common and proper nouns to writing, give each pair of students a plastic bag containing the "From Common to Proper" sentence strips. Have students place the strips facedown on their desks. Instruct them to take turns drawing a strip and orally replacing the underlined common nouns with proper nouns. Remind students that they may have to change the sentence slightly to make the new nouns properly fit the context. Invite students to share a few of their changes with the class.

Wrap-Up: Display page 4 of the Notebook file on the interactive whiteboard. Instruct students to listen carefully as you slowly read the paragraph aloud. Have students clap their hands twice when they see a common noun. If you touch the common nouns *(day, friend, street, pool, soda, lifeguard, seventh-graders, school, game, fun,* and *blast)* in this paragraph, you will hear the sound of clapping twice. After students have identified each common noun, have them turn to their partner and suggest a proper noun to replace it—one that makes sense and fits the context of the story. Students should be able to replace all the common nouns, except for *fun* and *blast*. Engage students in a discussion about the critical question.

A Writing Connection!

Display page 5 of the Notebook file on the interactive whiteboard. Ask students to write an original story using all of the common nouns listed in the order in which they appear. However, they must change these common nouns to proper nouns to make their writing more specific. When they have finished writing, put students in groups of four and have them read aloud their stories to one another.

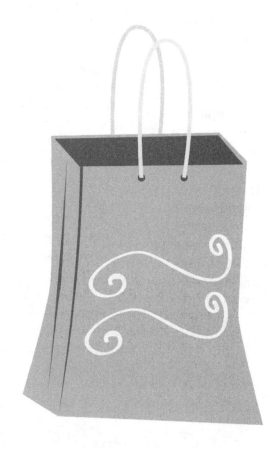

Name: _____ Date: _____

The Great Noun Race

Directions: Underline all the nouns in the sentences below.
(Hint: There are 31!)

On Saturday, Dana and Julia shopped at the Hampton Mall from

morning until night. First, they went to Airpostal, where they bought

matching Hawaiian print shirts. On the spot, the girls performed an

impromptu hula dance and attracted a huge crowd! Next, they searched

for an authentic grass skirt. Fortunately, around dinner time Julia and

Dana spotted Kyle Foster carrying a huge shopping bag filled with items

for Falcon Heights Middle School's Hawaiian Day. At PacMoon, he had

purchased an original hula skirt! Naturally, the two friends flew to the

boutique to purchase the rest of their outfit. Exhausted, the shoppers

hit Dairy King, where they ordered thick chocolate shakes to celebrate

their success.

From Common to Proper

At the <u>stadium</u>, a <u>baseball player</u> autographed my ball.

In the <u>summer months</u>, I love to vacation at the <u>beach</u>.

Cody refused to ride the <u>roller coaster</u> at the <u>amusement park</u>.

The <u>president</u> gave his speech at the capitol building in the <u>city</u>.

The <u>girl</u> hit a pothole with her <u>bicycle</u>.

My dad bought tickets from an <u>airline</u> to travel to an <u>island</u>.

I can't wait to see the <u>band</u> play at the <u>festival</u>.

My <u>dentist</u> recommended the best <u>toothpaste</u>.

On Tuesdays, I watch a TV <u>show</u> with my favorite <u>actor</u>.

I devoured a <u>candy bar</u> during the <u>movie</u>.

Lesson 10
Singular and Plural Nouns

Critical Question: How are singular and plural nouns written correctly?

You Need:

- "10 Singular and Plural Nouns" SMART Notebook file (on CD)

- "From One to Many" (page 47) — Make enough copies on cardstock for pairs of students. Laminate and cut apart the cards, then store each set of cards in a plastic bag.

- Dry-erase markers (for each pair of students)

- Paper towels

- Class copies of "Rules for Forming Plurals" (page 48)

- Class copies of "Practice With Plurals" (page 49)

- Class set of whiteboards, dry-erase markers, and erasers

Warm-Up: Display the SMART Notebook file titled "10 Singular and Plural Nouns" on the interactive whiteboard. Call on student volunteers to define the terms *singular* and *plural*. Then touch the words on the board to reveal their definitions. Touch the right arrow on the screen to go to the next page. Ask students: *What do you notice about the words in column one and in column two?* (The words in column one are singular, while the ones in column two are plural.)

What to Do:

1. Pair up students and give each pair a plastic bag containing the "From One to Many" cards, a dry-erase marker, and a paper towel. Ask partners to spread the cards on their desks and look for patterns

among the singular and plural word endings. Provide the following directions:

- Examine the word endings for both the singular and plural nouns.

- Group together the words that have similar patterns in their endings.

- Use the marker to circle the patterns.

Circulate through the room and ask students questions that lead them to discover the patterns.

2. In a whole-class discussion, invite students to share their categories and related words. Then, for each pattern they've discovered, have them state the rule for forming plurals of nouns in that category.

3. After students have shared their rules and the patterns they have discovered, distribute copies of "Rules for Forming Plurals." Have students record examples from their word sort under the corresponding rule on their sheets. Display page 3 of the Notebook file on the interactive whiteboard to show the first rule for forming plurals. Invite volunteers to come to the board and write examples of nouns that fit this rule. Touch the right arrow and repeat the process with each rule that follows. (Rules continue through page 10 of the Notebook file.)

4. Next, distribute whiteboards, dry-erase markers, and erasers to students. Then go to page 11 of the Notebook file. Instruct students to read the first sentence and, on their whiteboard, write the correct plural form of the word in parentheses.

When students have finished writing, ask them to show their answers at your signal. Students should then hold up their whiteboards. Call on a volunteer to use the eraser tool on the line to reveal the correct answer. Then ask partners to share with each other the rule they used to form the plural. Lower the screen shade to reveal another sentence and repeat the process. Sentences continue on the next page of the Notebook file.

5. Distribute copies of "Practice With Plurals" to students for additional reinforcement. Have students work on their sheets independently, then display page 13 of the Notebook file on the interactive whiteboard. Call on student volunteers to come to the board and drag the magnifying glass over the blanks to reveal the correct answers. Next, press the right arrow to display the paragraph with misspelled plurals. Drag the strawberry crate from the upper right-hand corner of the screen to its shadow on the left to see the correct spellings.

Wrap-Up: Display page 15 of the Notebook file on the interactive whiteboard. For each row of words invite a volunteer to come to the board and decide which is the correctly spelled plural. The correct word will spin, while the incorrect ones will disappear. Have seated students quietly discuss their choices with a partner before asking the volunteer to touch his or her answer. Repeat with the other rows of words.

A Writing Connection!

Have students write a postcard to a friend or relative describing a summer activity or a trip they have enjoyed. Ask them to include ten plural nouns that follow at least four different rules for forming plurals. Encourage students to illustrate their postcards and share them in groups of three or four.

From One to Many

pencil – pencils	clock – clocks
gas – gases	glass – glasses
brush – brushes	church – churches
box – boxes	buzz – buzzes
piano – pianos	taco – tacos
tomato – tomatoes	hero – heroes
baby – babies	country – countries
key – keys	turkey – turkeys
chief – chiefs	leaf – leaves
deer – deer	sheep – sheep
goose – geese	child – children

Rules for Forming Plurals

Rule 1: To form the plural of most nouns, just add *s*.

Examples: _____

Rule 2: When the singular noun ends in *s*, *ss*, *sh*, *ch*, *x*, or *z*, add *es*.

Examples: _____

Rule 3: When the singular ends in *o*, add *s* (except in: *echoes*, *heroes*, *potatoes*, *tomatoes*).

Examples: _____

Rule 4: When the singular ends in *y* with a consonant before it, change the *y* to *i* and add *es*.

Examples: _____

Rule 5: When the singular ends in *y* with a vowel before it, just add *s*.

Examples: _____

Rule 6: For some nouns ending in *f*, add *s*. For others, change the *f* to *v* and add *es* or *s*.

Examples: _____

Rule 7: Some nouns are the same for both singular and plural.

Examples: _____

Rule 8: Some nouns form their plurals in special ways.

Examples: _____

Practice With Plurals

Directions: Fill in the blank with the correct plural form of the singular noun.

1. How I love to watch the _____ sway in the summer breeze. *(birch)*

2. Their _____ flutter like graceful dancers. *(leaf)*

3. As I head out to pick _____, I hear the _____ honk. *(tomato / goose)*

4. In response, as if performing a duet, the wild _____ begin to gobble. *(turkey)*

5. Startled by the noise, two _____ drinking nectar take flight. *(butterfly)*

Directions: Underline and then correct the ten misspelled plurals in the paragraph below.

Throughout the summer, I take numerous journies in our garden.

In spite of the annoying mosquitos and soaring temperatures, I enjoy

harvesting strawberrys, squashies, and potatos. I put many of them in

wooden boxs to prepare them for market. If the vegetables are imperfect

because deers or insects have nibbled on them, I simply transport them

to one of the two dairys near our farm. While there, I often watch the cows

clean and nurture their newborn calfs. Sometimes I help the farmer shear

the sheeps. By the end of the day, I am exhausted from the work and the

heat, so I amble home for a cool, refreshing glass of iced tea.

Lesson 11
Possessive Nouns

Critical Question: How are possessive nouns correctly formed?

You Need:

- "11 Possessive Nouns" SMART Notebook file (on CD)
- Class copies of "Rule Sheet for Possessive Nouns" (page 52)
- Class copies of "Possessive Pennies" (page 53) — Cut out the word cards at the bottom of the page. For each student, put a set of cards in a plastic bag, along with 10 pennies with apostrophes taped to them and 10 pennies with the letter *s* taped to them.
- pennies
- tape
- Notebook paper
- Class copies of "Camping Rookies" (page 54)

Warm-Up: Display the SMART Notebook file titled "11 Possessive Nouns" on the interactive whiteboard. Direct students' attention to the first column on the chart and ask: *What do you notice about the words with apostrophes?* Guide them to notice that the words are singular nouns that show ownership. Use the eraser tool to erase the space above the column. Explain that nouns that show ownership are called *possessive nouns.* Ask: *By looking at these words, what do you think is the rule for forming singular possessives?* (Add an apostrophe and an *s* after the noun; for example, *story's plot*).

Next, drag the screen shade to the right to reveal the words in the second column. Erase the space above the column. Guide students to notice the pattern and discover the rule for forming plural possessives that end in *s*—simply add an apostrophe after the *s*; for example, *stories' plots.*

Singular Possessive	Plural Possessive	Irregular Plural Possessive
story's plot	stories' plots	children's shoes
city's park	cities' parks	men's pants
church's steeple	churches' steeples	deer's antlers
worker's lunch	workers' lunches	mice's cheese

Possessive nouns show ownership by using an _____ .

Reveal the third column to show students that to form irregular plural possessives, simply add an apostrophe and an *s* after the noun; for example, *children's shoes.* Erase the space above the column.

Touch inside the green box to reveal a statement about possessive nouns. Ask students to turn to a partner and discuss what word belongs on the blank line. Touch the space above the blank to reveal the word *apostrophe.*

What to Do:

1. Display page 2 of the Notebook file on the interactive whiteboard. Model how to create the singular possessive of the word *mother.* Drag the apostrophe and the *s* from inside the stars to form *mother's.* Call a volunteer to come to the board to create the singular possessive for *fish.* Invite seated students to use their finger to draw the "apostrophe *s*" in the air. Continue calling volunteers to the board until all the nouns have been changed to possessive nouns.

2. Distribute copies of "Rule Sheet for Possessive Nouns" to students, instructing them to take notes on the sheet. On the interactive whiteboard, drag on the purple PULL tab to reveal Rule #1: **Add an apostrophe s ('s) for singular nouns.** Have students copy the rule on their sheet and write their own examples of singular possessive nouns.

3. Touch the right arrow on the Notebook file to practice forming the possessives of

regular plural nouns. Invite a student to drag the apostrophe from inside the star to form *teachers'*. Repeat with the other words, then pull on the purple PULL tab to reveal Rule #2: **Add an apostrophe (') for plural nouns that end in s**. Have students copy the rule on their sheet and write their own examples.

4. Touch the right arrow to practice forming the possessives of irregular plural nouns (plural nouns that do not end in *s)*. Invite volunteers to the board to drag the apostrophe and the *s* to the nouns, then pull on the purple PULL tab to reveal Rule #3: **Add an apostrophe s ('s) for plural nouns that do not end in s**. Have students copy the rule and write examples on their sheet.

5. For a quick review of the strategy for forming possessives, go to page 5 of the Notebook file. Drag the screen shade down a bit to reveal the question students should first ask themselves when figuring out how to form a noun's possessive. Then drag down the screen shade some more to reveal the three rules students need to remember to form the possessives.

6. Touch the right arrow on the screen to provide mixed practice. Invite volunteers to go to the board and drag the apostrophe and the *s* from inside the stars to form the possessive nouns. Ask seated students to complete the same activity on their sheet.

7. Distribute the plastic bags containing the "Possessive Pennies" cards and pennies with apostrophes and *s* taped on them. Go to page 7 of the Notebook file to review the directions for the activity. When students have finished the activity, invite them to check each other's answers. (Answers will vary.)

Wrap-Up: Ask students to take out a sheet of paper, then display page 8 of the Notebook file on the interactive whiteboard. Have students read the first sentence on the board, then on their sheet, write the possessive form of the given noun. To check answers, call a volunteer to the board. Have the student orally share his or her response first, then drag the magnifying glass over the blank to reveal the correct answer. Repeat with the other sentences, which continue on page 9.

A Writing Connection!

To give students more practice with possessive nouns, distribute copies of "Camping Rookies." Have students underline and correct the ten possessive noun errors in the story. Then display pages 10 and 11 of the Notebook file on the interactive whiteboard. Invite volunteers to share their answers. Then drag the tent from the upper right-hand corner to its shadow on the left side to reveal the answers.

Rule Sheet for Possessive Nouns

Directions: In the chart below, copy each rule to form possessive nouns. Write four of your own examples for each possessive rule.

Rule #1: SINGULAR NOUNS	**Rule #2:** PLURAL NOUNS ending in *s*	**Rule #3:** PLURAL NOUNS *not* ending in *s*
EXAMPLES:	EXAMPLES:	EXAMPLES:

First, ask yourself: *Is it singular or plural?*

Second, remember the rules for possessives:

- If it is singular, add **'s**.
- If it is plural and ends in *s*, add an apostrophe (').
- If it is plural but does not end in *s*, add **'s**.

Directions: Add an apostrophe and/or *s* to create possessive nouns below.

1. elevator _____ buttons

2. geese _____ pond

3. athletes _____ uniforms

4. men _____ bathroom

5. lizard _____ tongue

6. deer _____ habitat

Possessive Pennies

CHART

sandwiches
Superman
brother
Joneses
students
clown
geese
babies
actors
children

books	**'**	**s**	**bottles**	**'**	**s**
lines	**'**	**s**	**hula hoop**	**'**	**s**
pickles	**'**	**s**	**cape**	**'**	**s**
games	**'**	**s**	**nose**	**'**	**s**
hamsters	**'**	**s**	**eggs**	**'**	**s**

Camping Rookies

Directions: Underline the ten possessive noun errors in the story below. Write the correct form of the possessive directly above the underlined word.

Last summer, my friend Liz and I decided to camp and backpack our way to Nova Scotia. Being unseasoned campers, we did not realize we were putting the tents' poles on the outside instead of the inside of the tent. Consequently, during a monsoon-like rainstorm, our tent collapsed, and our gear was totally waterlogged! We ended up sleeping in one of the parks' cabins.

In the morning, we visited the towns' Laundromat, where we placed our sleeping bags and clothes inside an enormous dryers' basket. Dressed in a neon-green T-shirt and striped pajama bottoms (her only dry clothes), Lizs' strange outfit attracted attention. In fact, two older ladies's mouths opened so wide, I thought their chins might hit their knees! Then, other peoples' whispers reached our ears.

"Look at those two rookies! They don't know the first thing about camping!" Embarrassed, our face's ivory skin quickly turned crimson.

Hungry from the morning activities, we decided to return to the campground to roast some hot dogs. When the Jones'es triplets yelled, "Boo!" from behind a bush, a frightened Liz dropped our lunch into the flames, and the hot dogs became firewood.

"Let's hope the fishs' appetites are hearty because it looks like we have to catch our lunch!" Liz shouted. As we headed for the stream, my stomach rumbled, and my wet sneakers sloshed. I thought to myself, "At least we have learned how to pitch a tent."

Lesson 12
Prepositions

Critical Question: What is a preposition?

You Need:

- "Parts of Speech Word Sort" (page 57) — Make enough copies on cardstock for pairs of students. Laminate and cut apart the cards, then store each set of cards in a plastic bag.
- Sticky notes
- "12 Prepositions" SMART Notebook file (on CD)
- Colorful T-shirt
- Index cards (four per student)
- Class copies of "Preposition Note Sheet" (page 58)
- Class copies of "The Preposition Song" (page 59)

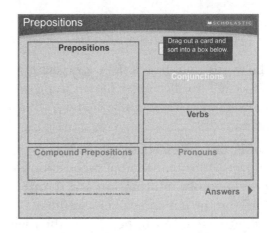

Warm-Up: Pair up students and give each pair a plastic bag containing the "Parts of Speech Word Sort" cards and some sticky notes. Ask partners to group the words into categories and to use the sticky notes to label the categories. Encourage students to look for patterns and to think about what they already know about parts of speech. After several minutes, invite students to share some of their categories and words. Then display the SMART Notebook file titled "12 Prepositions" on the interactive whiteboard to show some possible categories. Invite students to come to the board and drag out a word card and sort into the categories shown. Touch "Answers" to show how the word cards can be sorted.

What to Do:

1. Distribute copies of "Preposition Note Sheet" to students, telling them to use this sheet to take notes throughout the lesson. Display page 3 of the Notebook file on the interactive whiteboard. One by one, pull out the blue arrows from top to bottom up to the blue buttons. Tell students that the questions that appear will be answered in today's lesson.

2. Touch the top button next to the first question. Explain to students that prepositions are a part of speech. All the words we use belong to a certain part of speech, and each part of speech performs a particular job in a sentence. Explain that there are eight parts of speech in all, including prepositions. Invite a student volunteer to come to the board to touch the speech bubbles to reveal the other parts of speech. As each part of speech is revealed, ask students to give examples of that part of speech. Touch the home button to return to the questions page.

3. Explain that like the other parts of speech, prepositions have specific jobs. Touch the blue button next to the second question. On the new screen, lower the screen shade to show the first thing prepositions do— **show location**. Touch the illustration for an example. Invite students to act out the sentence on the board as you drag a preposition to the blank. For example, when you drag the word *near* to the blank, students should stand near their desks. When you place *against* on the blank, students should lean against their desks. Afterwards, touch the home button to see what else prepositions do.

4. Lower the screen shade to reveal another function of prepositions—**show time**. Touch the owl for an example. As you drag

the words into the blank, ask students how each word changes the meaning of the sentence. Then touch the home button again.

5. Lower the screen shade all the way to show the third function of prepositions — **provide more information and detail**. Click on the girl and call on a student volunteer to come to the front of the room. Hand him or her a brightly colored T-shirt. Ask the student to act out the sentence on the board as you drag a preposition to the blank. Start with the word *in* and ask the student to put on the shirt. Then replace *in* with *with* and have the student take off the shirt and stand with it. Touch the home button to return to the questions.

6. Ask students: *Now that we know what prepositions do, why should we use them in our writing?* Touch the button next to the third question. Pull down the screen shade and read the first sample sentence. Point out that the sentence has no preposition. Then pull down the screen shade all the way to reveal the sentence with a preposition. Click above the dancing kids to reveal the tent. Have students turn to their partner and discuss the question at the top of the screen. Then invite them to share their ideas with the class.

7. On the next page of the Notebook file, challenge students to find the prepositions in each sentence. Call on a student volunteer to come to the board and find the two prepositions in the first sentence. If the student touches the correct word, he or she will hear "correct." Invite another volunteer to find the two prepositions in the second sentence.

8. Ask students: *How many prepositions do you need to learn?* Display page 11 of the Notebook file. Touch the speech bubble to reveal the number (49).

9. The next page lists all 49 prepositions in alphabetical order. Click on each box to reveal one column at a time, encouraging students to memorize the words in each column. Explain to students that one way to help memorize all 49 prepositions is to chunk them and put them in a song.

10. Distribute copies of "The Preposition Song" to students. Display page 13 of the Notebook and touch the cowboy hat to launch a music video of students singing "The Preposition Song." Play the video a few times until students become familiar with the tune. Then invite them to sing the first verse one line at a time, repeating each line several times until students can sing it well. You may want to teach one verse at a time and to quiz students on each verse. To demonstrate mastery, they can then sing or write all 49 words in the song.

Wrap-Up: Display page 14 of the Notebook file on the interactive whiteboard. Invite volunteers to the board to sort the words into the correct column. Discuss with the class whether or not each choice is correct.

Next, distribute four index cards to each student, telling students to label the cards with a large capital A, B, C, and D. Then go to page 15 of the Notebook file for a multiple choice review. Invite a student volunteer to come to the board and read the first sentence aloud. After students view and listen to the sentence, ask them to identify the preposition by holding up the index card with the letter of the correct answer. To ensure students do not piggyback on their classmates' answers, provide a verbal signal (such as "Show me now") before they reveal their answers. Ask the volunteer to touch the letter of the correct answer to check. The correct answer will spin. Pull down the screen shade to show the next sentence. Continue until all sentences have been revealed.

Parts of Speech Word Sort

along	during	of	with
from	at	between	instead of
in front of	but	and	we
them	over	toward	be
had	so	beneath	on top of
down	like	not only	until

Preposition Note Sheet

What is a part of speech?

• A _____ in our English language that has a certain job in a sentence.

• The eight parts of speech are _____, _____,

_____, _____, _____,

_____, _____, and _____.

What do prepositions do?

• Prepositions _____, _____, and

_____

• List all 49 prepositions here:

The Preposition Song
(to the tune of "Yankee Doodle")

Above / about / across / after

along / among / around / at

before / beside / between / against

within / without / beneath / through

CHORUS

During / under / in / into

over / off / of / to / toward

up / on / near / for / from / except

by / with / behind / below / down.

In front of / inside / instead of

like / on top of / onto / out

outside / past / since / underneath

until / upon / YEAH, WAHOO!

REPEAT CHORUS

Lesson 13
Prepositional Phrases

Critical Question: What is a prepositional phrase?

You Need:

- "13 Prepositional Phrases" SMART Notebook file (on CD)
- Plain white paper (one per student)
- Scissors (for each student)
- Whiteboards, dry-erase markers, erasers
- 8½" x 11" white construction paper
- Class copies of "Find the Prepositional Phrases" (page 62)
- Class copies of "Preposition Treasure Hunt" (page 63)
- Class copies of "Treasure Hunt Rubric" (page 64)

Warm-Up: Display the SMART Notebook file titled "13 Prepositional Phrases" on the interactive whiteboard. Have students read the phrases on the screen and identify the prepositions. Ask: *Do the phrases make sense on their own?* (No) Call on a volunteer to drag a picture from the bottom of the screen and place it at the end of the first phrase. Then have the student "read" the phrase by naming the noun the picture represents. Repeat with other student volunteers until all the phrases make sense. Then ask students to turn to a partner and tell each other what part of speech must be used after a preposition to create a *prepositional phrase* (a noun or pronoun).

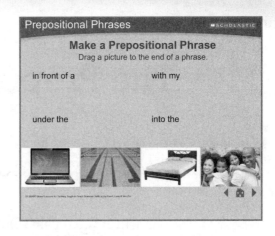

What to Do:

1. Distribute a piece of plain paper and a pair of scissors to each student. Tell students that they will be making a note-taking foldable. Model how to make one by first folding the paper in half the long way, then folding it again two more times to divide the sheet into eight parts, as shown. Open the paper. Holding the paper horizontally, cut along each fold (indicated by dashes) down to the center fold to make four flaps. Then fold the paper in half again so the flaps face up. Tell students that they will be using the foldable to take notes during this lesson.

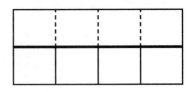

2. Explain to students that in order for a preposition to become a phrase, it needs an *object*. The object of a preposition can be any one of four things. Display page 2 of the Notebook file on the interactive whiteboard and point to the word *Nouns* on the chart. On the first flap of the foldable, have students write the word *Nouns*. Touch the cell below to reveal the example. Under the first flap of the foldable, have students copy the example exactly as it appears in the box.

3. To reinforce the concept, touch the Practice button below the Nouns column. Read aloud the sentence: *I enjoy skiing in the winter.* Point out the preposition (in red) and its object (in blue). Invite a volunteer to the board to drag a

red preposition, a black article, and a blue object to the box below to create a prepositional phrase. Then tell the volunteer to use the SMART pen to circle the preposition and box the object. Call on two more students to create additional prepositional phrases. Then touch the home button to return to the chart.

4. Touch the top of the second column to reveal the next object: *Pronouns*. Instruct students to write the word on the second flap of their foldable. Then touch the cell below to show an example for students to copy in the space under the second flap. Press the Practice button to show a sentence with a prepositional phrase that uses a pronoun as its object. Again, invite student volunteers to the board to create prepositional phrases by dragging the red and blue words to the large box below. Touch the home button to return to the chart.

5. Repeat Steps 3 and 4 to introduce the remaining objects of prepositions—compounds and modifiers—noting the addition of conjunctions and descriptive words.

6. To assess students' understanding, distribute whiteboards, dry-erase markers, and erasers. Display page 7 of the Notebook file on the interactive whiteboard. Pull down the screen shade to reveal a prepositional phrase. For each phrase revealed, have students write the object on their whiteboard. Then at your signal, have students hold up their whiteboards to show their answers. Drag the screen shade down to reveal additional phrases. Collect the materials at the end of the activity.

7. For independent practice, distribute copies of "Find the Prepositional Phrases" to students. Have students work on their sheet independently, following the directions to complete the activity. When students have finished, display page 8 of the Notebook file. Invite volunteers to come to the board and touch the correct prepositional phrases to reveal the answers. (Sentences continue on page 9.)

Wrap-Up: Divide the class into groups of four, and give each group one whiteboard, one dry-erase marker, and one eraser. Appoint a scorekeeper for each group who will record group members' names and the score on a piece of paper. Tell students that they will be playing the "Name That Phrase!" game. Display page 10 of the Notebook file on the interactive whiteboard, and pull down the screen shade to reveal a sentence that contains one or more prepositional phrases. Each group quietly decides what the phrase is, and one person writes it on the whiteboard, circles the preposition, and boxes the object. Rotate the "recorder" job as each sentence is revealed so all group members participate. The teams take turns sending a group member to the board to the touch the prepositional phrase. (A recorded voice will let students know if they are correct.) The student then orally identifies the preposition and its object. If correct, the team receives two points. Other teams that have the correct answer receives one point. Sentences continue on page 11 of the Notebook file. Emphasize that if teams are too loud, have poor sportsmanship, or misuse materials, they lose a point. At the end of the game, the team with the most points wins.

A Writing Connection!

To demonstrate the importance of using prepositional phrases in writing, distribute copies of "Preposition Treasure Hunt" and "Treasure Hunt Rubric" to students for homework. Go over the directions and rubric to acquaint students with the expectations for the assignment. Emphasize that they need to choose a "theme" for their map. For example, some students might choose to create "Soccer Island," while others might choose ice cream or music as their theme.

Find the Prepositional Phrases

Directions: Identify the prepositional phrases in the sentences. **UNDERLINE** the entire prepositional phrase, then **CIRCLE** the preposition and **BOX** the object. Use the preposition song to help you find the prepositions/ prepositional phrases in each of the sentences.

Example: I am (on) the football [team].

1. We will sing a duet for the talent show.

2. During the dance, Mark spun Vanessa around the floor.

3. Carly will play the national anthem on the piano at the football game tonight.

4. Behind the desk under the chair, you will find my tap shoes.

5. Since this morning, I have gone to the bathroom six times!

6. Cody is sulking down the hallway and into the principal's office.

7. At the game, Elizabeth booted the football into the goal!

8. Hannah swam with the dolphins in the crystal clear water of the Caribbean.

9. Throughout the night, dreams whirled inside my head.

10. According to our coach, our team ranks highest above the others.

Preposition Treasure Hunt

Arrrgghh, matey! Ye better follow directions on this here assignment, or ye might find yerself walkin' the plank!

1. Create a treasure map on an 8½" x 11" piece of white construction paper. The map should be large enough to cover the paper completely and should be neatly colored. On the map, include the following:

   • A compass rose

   • 7 landforms and other physical features—such as cliffs, mountains, bridges, and bodies of water—with unique names that relate to the theme of your map

   • Important places, such as Skeleton Mountain or Wailing Woods, that are clearly labeled

   Do NOT draw dotted lines OR write an "X" where the treasure is located.

2. On a separate sheet of paper write a clear set of directions that will lead the treasure hunter to the location of the treasure. Write a minimum of ten complete sentences. Each sentence must contain one <u>underlined</u> prepositional phrase. (If the sentence has more than one prepositional phrase, underline only one.) At least ten different prepositions should be used. Make sure you include a variety of sentences in your directions. Do not start all sentences in the same way. Below are two examples of what you might write:

   > *To find King Harry's treasure, follow these directions:*
   >
   > **1.** *Head due north* **<u>toward</u>** <u>*Goblin Gulch*</u>*.*
   >
   > **2. At** *Goblin Gulch, gather the skull bones* **in** *your backpack and travel* **<u>around</u>** <u>*the west side*</u> **of** *the gulch* **to** *Skeleton Mountain.*

3. In class, you will exchange your map with a partner, who will use your directions to locate the treasure. If your partner finds the location of your treasure without your assistance, both of you will earn bonus points!

Name: _____ Date: _____

Treasure Hunt Rubric

Criteria for Evaluation	Advanced 4	Proficient 3	Basic 2	Below Basic 1
The directions are written with a variety of sentence starters and in complete sentences. _____ (score)	All sentences are complete and have a unique beginning.	Most sentences have a unique beginning and/or most are complete sentences.	Some sentences have a unique beginning and/or some are complete sentences.	Few sentences have a unique beginning and/or few are complete sentences.
There are at least 10 sentences, and each sentence contains at least one underlined prepositional phrase. _____ (score)	There are at least 10 sentences, and all sentences contain at least one underlined prepositional phrase.	There are 8 or 9 sentences and/or most sentences contain at least one underlined prepositional phrase.	There are only 7 sentences and/or some sentences contain at least one underlined prepositional phrase.	There are fewer than 7 sentences and/or only a few sentences contain at least one underlined prepositional phrase.
Ten different prepositions are used correctly. _____ (score)	All 10 underlined prepositions differ from one another and are used correctly.	8 or 9 underlined prepositions differ from one another and/or most are used correctly.	7 underlined prepositions differ from one another and/or some are used correctly.	Fewer than 7 underlined prepositions differ from one another and/or only a few are used correctly.
Map contains a compass, 7 landforms, other physical features and/or places, which are clearly labeled and relate to the map's theme. _____ (score)	The map has a compass. Seven different labeled features clearly relate to the theme.	The map has a compass. Five or six different labeled features clearly relate to the theme.	The map may or may not have a compass. Three or four different labeled features clearly relate to the theme.	The map may or may not have a compass. Few features are labeled and/or do not relate to the theme.
Map is neat, colorful, and is drawn in proportion to the size of the paper. _____ (score)	The map is extraordinarily neat and colorful; it fills the page and is drawn in proportion.	The map is neat, colorful, uses space well, and is close to the right size.	The map is somewhat neat and colorful; there is too much white space. The drawing is somewhat disproportionate to the page size.	The map is not neat or colorful. It is not drawn in proportion to the size of the paper.

Total Score: _____/20

Lesson 14

Elaborating With Prepositional Phrases

Critical Question: How can I use prepositional phrases to add more description to my writing?

You Need:

• "14 Elaborating With Prepositions" SMART Notebook file (on CD)

• Class copies of "Before and After" (pages 67–68)

• Index cards

Warm-Up: Display the SMART Notebook file titled "14 Elaborating With Prepositions" on the interactive whiteboard. Read aloud the statement at the top of the page. Guide students to notice that both the sample sentence and the girl seem somewhat plain. Ask students to think about a prepositional phrase to add detail to the noun *girl*. Then, click on the girl to change the color of her dress and shoes. Invite a student volunteer to come to the board and move the word *smiles* and the period. Then have him or her use the SMART pen to add a prepositional phrase right after the word *girl*. Remind the student to drag the word *smiles* and the period back to complete the sentence.

Touch the right arrow to go to the next page. Read aloud the statement at the top of the page, then ask students to think about a prepositional phrase to describe the verb *wiggles* in the sentence underneath. Touch the boy icon to play a video. After watching how William wiggles, call on a volunteer to come to the board, move the period, and use the pen to write a prepositional phrase that provides more information about how, where, or when William wiggles.

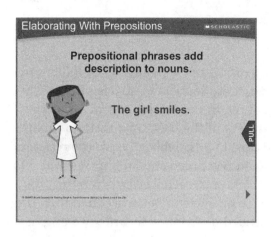

What to Do:

1. Display page 3 of the Notebook file on the interactive whiteboard. Tell students that each sentence could use more description. Invite a student volunteer to come to the board to drag a prepositional phrase from the box at the bottom and add it after each noun in the first sentence. Remind the student to move the words and punctuation to expand the sentence. Call on two other volunteers to work on the other sentences.

2. Touch the right arrow to go to the next page. This time, invite student volunteers to move the prepositional phrases to describe the verbs in each sentence.

3. For more practice, distribute copies of "Before and After" to students. Have students read the "plain" sentence in the middle column and, in the "Before" column, draw a picture of what they see. Next, tell students to add a prepositional phrase to expand the sentence. Then instruct them to draw an "after" picture to show how the elaboration changes the sentence's meaning. When students are finished, ask them to fold their papers so that the "Before" and "After" columns are next to each other. Pair up students, then tell them to guess what prepositional phrase their partner added based on the "Before" and "After" pictures. Prompt them to discuss how the pictures model the importance of prepositional phrases in writing.

Wrap-Up: Give each student an index card. Instruct students to write one noun at the top of the front of the card and one verb at the top of the back. Ask them to "mail" the card to a "neighbor." Have the recipient write in two prepositional phrases that add description to each word, then return the card to its owner. The owner then uses the expanded description to write two original sentences. Have students share the new sentences with a different neighbor.

A Writing Connection!

Challenge students to write an advertisement to sell an object of their choice. The ad must contain ten prepositional phrases. Five of the phrases must modify (describe) nouns, while the other five must modify verbs. To make checking for accuracy fast and easy, tell students to highlight the prepositional phrases modifying nouns in yellow and the ones modifying verbs in pink.

Before and After

Directions: For each of the following sentences, draw a picture in the "Before" column that represents the content of the sentence without a prepositional phrase. Then, on the lines provided, add a prepositional phrase to the noun/verb (as indicated) and draw a picture in the "After" column to represent the improved sentence.

BEFORE		AFTER
	(noun) **1.** The <u>clown</u> sat and shared his ice cream. _____ _____ _____	
	(noun) **2.** The <u>butterfly</u> carelessly floated. _____ _____ _____	
	(find the noun) **3.** His book sold out. _____ _____ _____	

(continued)

Before and After (continued)

BEFORE		AFTER
	(verb) **4.** Megan's voice <u>squeaked</u>. _____ _____	
	(verb) **5.** That dog <u>growled</u>. _____ _____ _____	
	(find the verb) **6.** Tim swallowed the juicy bug. _____ _____	
	(both noun and verb) **7.** The <u>water</u> <u>dripped</u>. _____ _____ _____	

Lesson 15
Varying Sentence Beginnings

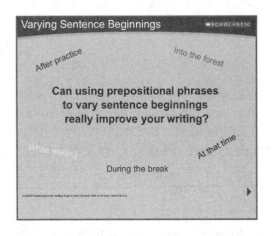

Critical Question: How do I use prepositional phrases to vary my sentence beginnings?

You Need:

- "15 Varying Sentence Beginnings" SMART Notebook file (on CD)
- Class copies of "Cut & Paste Prepositions" (page 71)
- Construction paper
- Scissors
- Glue sticks

Warm-Up: Display the SMART Notebook file titled "15 Varying Sentence Beginnings" on the interactive whiteboard and invite a student to read aloud the question on the first page. Tell students that you are going to read aloud two paragraphs on the same subject. Ask them to listen carefully so they can decide which paragraph they think sounds better.

Touch the right arrow to go to the first paragraph. Since all of the sentences in this paragraph start with the subject, use your voice to project the flat monotone that boring writing produces.

Next, touch the right arrow on the screen to go to the next paragraph. Several sentences in this paragraph start with a prepositional phrase (highlighted in green), so reflect the lively nature of this paragraph with your voice. Afterward, ask students to choose the better paragraph and to provide reasons for their responses. Guide them to discover how using prepositional phrases to add sentence variety makes writing much more interesting to read. Also, point out how prepositional phrases in the second

paragraph help connect one idea to another. Emphasize that prepositional phrases not only create style in writing but also enhance organization.

What to Do:

1. Explain to students that one way to create sentence variety is to start a sentence with a prepositional phrase. Go to page 4 of the Notebook file and read the first sentence. Explain that while this is a perfectly good sentence, you can make it more interesting by moving phrases around. Touch and drag the phrase "into the bowl" and move it in front of the subject "I," then adjust the rest of the sentence to fit. Use the SMART pen to add editing marks to fix capitalization.

2. Pull down the screen shade to reveal each sentence one at a time. For each sentence, call on a volunteer to come to the board and drag the prepositional phrase in front of the subject and rearrange the remaining words in the sentence to form a complete thought. Then touch "Answers" to check students' responses.

3. Distribute copies of "Cut & Paste Prepositions" to students, along with a piece of construction paper, scissors, and glue. Ask students to cut out the words and phrases and use them to create ten sentences that start with a prepositional phrase, are complete thoughts, and make sense. After students manipulate the words and phrases, have partners check each other's work. Then have them glue their sentences to the construction paper.

4. To show some possible combinations for sentences, display page 6 of the Notebook file on the interactive whiteboard. Emphasize that using prepositional phrases to begin a sentence adds style and variety to writing.

Wrap-Up: Ask students to write a five-sentence paragraph. Each sentence must contain a prepositional phrase and start with the subject. Tell students to skip lines as they write. Then ask them to exchange paragraphs with a partner, who will revise it by starting two or three of the sentences with a prepositional phrase. Afterward, have students discuss how varying sentence beginnings with prepositional phrases can improve their writing. (Of course, remind them that starting *every* sentence with a prepositional phrase when they are writing can also get boring.)

A Writing Connection!

Ask students to select a past piece of writing to revise. Have them highlight only the prepositional phrases that start sentences and tally the number of sentences that start with a prepositional phrase. Then have them count the other sentences in the piece and compare the results. If few sentences begin with a prepositional phrase, have students revise several of the sentences. Ask them to start these sentences with an appropriate prepositional phrase. Remind students that they may need to add and/or delete words as they change the sentence beginnings.

Cut & Paste Prepositions

the students	five miles	on the counter	are reading	my brother	boiled
down the lane	ate	for our laptop	wrestled	vibrated	after dinner
in the morning	in the bedroom	my family	its paws	macaroni	the bowling ball
a new printer	licks	bought	I	the cell phone	threw
pillows	Dad	ran	rolled	with its tongue	we
the cat	on the stove	at a restaurant	Cody and Liam	during class	a large meal

Professional References

Dorfman, L. & Capelli, R. (2007). *Mentor texts: Teaching writing through children's literature K-6.* Portland: Stenhouse Publishers.

Harrison III, H.L., & Hummell, L.J. (2010). Incorporating animation concepts and principles in STEM education. *Technology Teacher*, 69(8), 20-25.

Irvin, J.L., Meltzer, J., & Dukes, M.S. (2007). *Taking action on adolescent literacy.* Alexandria, VA: Association for Supervision & Curriculum Development.

Jensen, E. (2000). Moving with the brain in mind. *Educational Leadership*, 18(1), 34-38.

Madrazo, G., Jr., & Motz, L. (2005). Brain research: Implications to diverse learners. *Science Educator* 14(1), 56-60.

Marzano, R.J. (2003). *What works in schools.* Alexandria, VA: Association for Supervision & Curriculum Development.

Marzano, R.J. (2007). *The art and science of teaching.* Alexandria, VA: Association for Supervision & Curriculum Development.

Marzano, R.J. (2009). Teaching with interactive whiteboards. *Multiple Measures*, 67(3), 80-82.

Marzano, R.J., & Haystead, M.W. (Ed.). (2009). *Evaluation study of the effects of Promethean active classroom on student achievement.* Marzano Research Laboratory, Powered by Solution Tree.

Marzano, R.J. (2010). Summarizing to comprehend. *Educational Leadership*, 67(6), 83-84.

On the lexical fringe. (2007). *School Library Journal*, 53(5), 29.

Polette. K. (2008). *Teaching grammar through writing: Activities to develop writer's craft in all students grades 4-12.* Boston: Pearson Education, Inc.

Powell, K.C., & Kalina, C.J. (2009). Cognitive and social constructivism: Developing tools for an effective classroom. *Education*, 130(2), 241-250.

Smart technologies K-12 case studies. (2010). Retrieved from http://education.smarttech. com/ste/en-US/News+and+research/Case+studies+and+best+practices/K-12+case+studies/

Stevens-Smith, D. (2004). Movement and learning: A valuable connection. *Strategies*, 18(1), 10-12.